STATE PROFILES
COLORADO

BY NATHAN SOMMER

BELLWETHER MEDIA • MINNEAPOLIS, MN

Blastoff! Discovery launches a new mission: reading to learn. Filled with facts and features, each book offers you an exciting new world to explore!

BLASTOFF! UNIVERSE

BLASTOFF! Beginners — GRADE K

BLASTOFF! READERS — GRADES 1-3

BLASTOFF! DISCOVERY — GRADE 4

This edition first published in 2022 by Bellwether Media, Inc.

No part of this publication may be reproduced in whole or in part without written permission of the publisher.
For information regarding permission, write to Bellwether Media, Inc., Attention: Permissions Department,
6012 Blue Circle Drive, Minnetonka, MN 55343.

Library of Congress Cataloging-in-Publication Data

Names: Sommer, Nathan, author.
Title: Colorado / by Nathan Sommer.
Description: Minneapolis, MN : Bellwether Media, Inc., 2022. | Series: Blastoff! Discovery: State profiles | Includes bibliographical references and index. | Audience: Ages 7-13 | Audience: Grades 4-6 | Summary: "Engaging images accompany information about Colorado. The combination of high-interest subject matter and narrative text is intended for students in grades 3 through 8"– Provided by publisher.
Identifiers: LCCN 2021019656 (print) | LCCN 2021019657 (ebook) | ISBN 9781644873779 (library binding) | ISBN 9781648341540 (ebook)
Subjects: LCSH: Colorado–Juvenile literature.
Classification: LCC F776.3 .S675 2022 (print) | LCC F776.3 (ebook) | DDC 978.8–dc23
LC record available at https://lccn.loc.gov/2021019656
LC ebook record available at https://lccn.loc.gov/2021019657

Editor: Kate Moening   Designer: Brittany McIntosh

Printed in the United States of America, North Mankato, MN.

TABLE OF CONTENTS

WELCOME TO COLORADO!	4
WHERE IS COLORADO?	6
COLORADO'S BEGINNINGS	8
LANDSCAPE AND CLIMATE	10
WILDLIFE	12
PEOPLE AND COMMUNITIES	14
DENVER	16
INDUSTRY	18
FOOD	20
SPORTS AND ENTERTAINMENT	22
FESTIVALS AND TRADITIONS	24
COLORADO TIMELINE	26
COLORADO FACTS	28
GLOSSARY	30
TO LEARN MORE	31
INDEX	32

CHASM LAKE
ROCKY MOUNTAIN NATIONAL PARK

A family takes their first steps into Rocky Mountain National Park. Before them, Longs Peak rises into the clear blue sky. They spot several bighorn sheep on the mountain's snowy slopes. Along their hiking trail are bright Colorado blue columbine, the state's official flower.

GARDEN OF THE GODS

GREAT SAND DUNES NATIONAL PARK

MESA VERDE CLIFF DWELLINGS

RED ROCKS AMPHITHEATRE

After a long hike, the family stops at Chasm Lake at the mountain's base. They are tired, but the view makes the journey worth it. Welcome to Colorado! The adventure has just begun.

UTAH

ARIZONA

Square-shaped Colorado sits in the western United States on the edge of the **Great Plains**. It covers 104,094 square miles (269,602 square kilometers). Wyoming borders Colorado to the north. Nebraska hugs the northeastern corner. Kansas sits to the east. Oklahoma and New Mexico make up Colorado's southern border. Arizona touches Colorado's southwestern corner at Four Corners. Utah is on the state's western edge.

The Rocky Mountains tower over Colorado's western half. The capital city, Denver, lies to the east of the Rockies. The state is named after the Colorado River that flows through its northwestern corner.

WYOMING

NEBRASKA

FORT COLLINS

BOULDER

COLORADO
RIVER

DENVER

AURORA

COLORADO

COLORADO
SPRINGS

KANSAS —

PUEBLO

OKLAHOMA

NEW
MEXICO

ALL IN A NAME

Colorado is a Spanish word that means "colored red." Spanish explorers named the Colorado River for its red soil!

COLORADO GOLD RUSH

GROCERY

Native Americans have lived in Colorado for at least 11,000 years. The Puebloan people were among the earliest residents. Later, the Ute people made homes in the Colorado mountains. The Arapaho, Comanche, and Cheyenne traveled Colorado's Great Plains.

Gold-seeking Spanish settlers first explored Colorado in the late 1500s. The United States bought part of Colorado in the **Louisiana Purchase** of 1803. The rest was given to the United States in 1848 after the Mexican-American War. In the late 1850s, the **gold rush** took the nation by storm! Americans flocked to the state. Colorado became the 38th state on August 1, 1876.

NATIVE PEOPLES OF COLORADO

SOUTHERN UTE

- Original lands in Colorado's south-central mountains
- Around 1,400 in Colorado today
- Also called Mouache and Caputa

UTE MOUNTAIN UTE

- Original lands in southwestern corner of the state
- Around 2,100 in Colorado today
- Also called Weenuchiu and Weeminuche

Colorado is the only state completely above 3,281 feet (1,000 meters) of **elevation**. The forested Rocky Mountains blanket Colorado's western half. Farmland and prairies stretch across the Great Plains in eastern Colorado. The dry desert of the Colorado **Plateau** makes up much of southwestern Colorado.

COLORADO PLATEAU   GREAT PLAINS
ROCKY MOUNTAINS

GREAT PLAINS

ROCKY MOUNTAINS

ROCKY MOUNTAIN SNOW

It snows in the Rocky Mountains during every season. Some areas get more than 35 feet (10.7 meters) of snow each year!

SPRING
HIGH: 62°F (17°C)
LOW: 33°F (1°C)

SUMMER
HIGH: 85°F (29°C)
LOW: 54°F (12°C)

FALL
HIGH: 64°F (18°C)
LOW: 33°F (1°C)

WINTER
HIGH: 42°F (6°C)
LOW: 14°F (-10°C)

°F = degrees Fahrenheit
°C = degrees Celsius

Colorado's eastern plains have hot summers and cool, dry winters. The Rockies are wetter and colder year-round. Snowy winters bring blizzards to many parts of the state. Valleys beneath the Rockies experience **flash floods** in the spring as mountain snow melts.

11

AMERICAN PIKA

Colorado's Rocky Mountains are home to thousands of plants and animals. Tiny pikas hide in rock piles high in the mountains. Furry marmots scurry nearby. Elk, deer, and bighorn sheep climb to feed on mountain plants. They keep a watchful eye for hungry lynx, grizzly bears, and gray wolves.

CANADA LYNX

Prairie dogs share their tunnels with burrowing owls in Colorado's eastern plains. Skinks also hide underground. Red foxes, wild turkeys, and pronghorn roam above ground. They hide their young from golden eagles that attack from above.

GOLDEN EAGLE

GREAT PLAINS SKINK

PRONGHORN

BIGHORN SHEEP

Life Span: up to 15 years
Status: least concern

bighorn sheep range =

LEAST CONCERN	NEAR THREATENED	VULNERABLE	ENDANGERED	CRITICALLY ENDANGERED	EXTINCT IN THE WILD	EXTINCT

More than 5.7 million Coloradans call the state home. Denver and the cities around it make up more than half of Colorado's population. This is one of the fastest-growing areas in the United States! The Rocky Mountains have smaller populations than the busy Denver area. In some parts, there is only one person per 1 square mile (2.6 square kilometers)!

COLORADO'S FUTURE: WATER SHORTAGE

With Colorado's population growing so quickly, many worry that soon there will not be enough water for everyone. Communities are already taking steps to conserve water. But the changes in Earth's climate will continue to increase the problem.

FORT COLLINS

White Americans are the largest group in Colorado. Hispanic Americans are the next-largest group. There are smaller numbers of Asian Americans and Black or African Americans. Much of Colorado's Native American population lives around Denver and Colorado Springs.

DENVER

COLORADO'S CHALLENGE: HOUSING CRISIS

Denver's population is growing fast. This is causing housing prices to go up. It is getting harder for middle- and lower-income families to afford housing. This will lead to more homelessness and a bigger divide between rich and poor.

Denver is called the Mile High City. It sits exactly 1 mile (1.6 kilometers) above sea level. The city has been Colorado's capital since before it was a state! It was a major **hub** of the Wild West's fur trade and mining industries.

Today, Denver residents love to get outside. The peaks of 200 mountains can be seen from downtown Denver! The city has many flower gardens and more than 200 public parks. It is also one of the only cities in the country with eight professional sports teams.

LOGGING

Early Colorado was built on the Wild West's gold mining. Later, the logging and railroad industries helped the area grow. Petroleum, natural gas, and coal mining are important parts of the economy today.

AIR FORCE ACADEMY

The United States Air Force Academy is in Colorado Springs. It trains around 4,000 cadets at a time!

Colorado has some of the country's lowest **unemployment** rates. Most people work in **service jobs**. Many work for large technology companies near Denver. Google and Facebook both have **campuses** in the area. Others provide for the many **tourists** that visit the state. Farming remains important in Colorado's eastern plains. Livestock, machinery, and medical tools are the state's biggest **exports**.

INVENTED IN COLORADO

JOLLY RANCHERS
Date Invented: 1949
Inventors: Bill and Dorothy Harmsen

RECYCLABLE ALUMINUM CAN
Date Invented: 1959
Inventor: William Coors

CHIPOTLE MEXICAN GRILL
Date Invented: first opened in 1993
Inventor: Steve Ells

CROCS
Date Invented: 2002
Inventors: Lyndon Hanson, Scott Seamans, and George Boedecker Jr.

GRILLED
LAMB

COLORADO-STYLE PIZZA

Colorado has its own type of pizza. Colorado-style pizza has a thick, braided crust, often made with honey. Coloradans may also dip their crusts in honey for dessert!

Many Colorado recipes feature livestock from the state's eastern plains. Some say Colorado lamb is the country's best! People love to make burgers and sausage from local elk and bison. They enjoy fresh trout from Rocky Mountain rivers.

Colorado's famous ingredient is the green chile. Puebloan peoples have cooked using these peppers for centuries. Today, Coloradans mix them into chili and top burgers or burritos with them. Colorado is also famous for its peaches. **Farmers markets** around the state showcase fresh juices made from these as well as other fruits such as melons.

BISON BURGER

PEACHES

COLORADO GREEN CHILI

8-10 SERVINGS

Have an adult help you make this popular chili!

INGREDIENTS

2 pounds cubed pork
1 tablespoon garlic
1/4 teaspoon pepper
3 tablespoons flour
1 can diced tomatoes

1 can chicken broth
1 cup water
20 green chiles
tortilla chips, sour cream, or cheese for toppings

DIRECTIONS

1. Cook the pork in a skillet with garlic and pepper. Add the flour and cook until brown.

2. Dice the green chiles.

3. Mix the pork, tomatoes, chicken broth, water, and green chiles in a pot. Simmer for at least two hours. Add water to make it thinner or flour to make it thicker.

4. Add whatever toppings you'd like. Enjoy!

WHITEWATER RAFTING

Coloradans seek adventure in every season. In warmer months, they hike, bike, or kayak in Rocky Mountain National Park. Brave Coloradans rock climb or go whitewater rafting. In winter, skiers from around the world flock to destinations including Vail and Aspen.

SKIING

Denver residents gather in its many parks to have picnics or watch plays. Many attend concerts at the Red Rocks **Amphitheatre**. Colorado has a team for every major professional sport. The Colorado Avalanche have won the Stanley Cup twice. The Denver Broncos have won the Super Bowl three times!

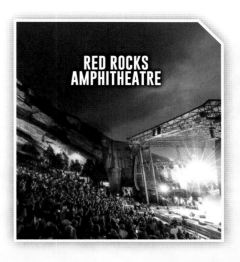

RED ROCKS AMPHITHEATRE

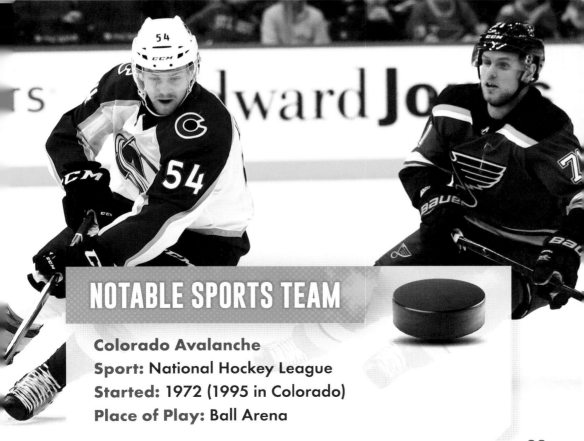

NOTABLE SPORTS TEAM

Colorado Avalanche
Sport: National Hockey League
Started: 1972 (1995 in Colorado)
Place of Play: Ball Arena

RACING WITH DONKEYS!

Several Colorado festivals include pack burro racing. This wacky sport began during Colorado's mining days. During Fairplay's Burro Days, humans and donkeys race side-by-side for nearly 30 miles (48 kilometers)!

Coloradans love to celebrate their Wild West **heritage**. Thousands attend the Colorado State Fair in Pueblo each August to watch horseback riding or rodeos. Others bring big appetites to taste spicy peppers at Pueblo's Chile and Frijoles Festival.

Locals love winter, too. Each January, climbers from across the world climb frozen waterfalls at the Ouray Ice Festival. In Breckenridge, teams of ice sculptors craft frozen works of art during the International Snow Sculpting Championship. Sunshine or snow, Coloradans always seek adventure in their state!

OURAY ICE FESTIVAL

1874

The U.S. government takes away Ute lands after the signing of the Brunot Agreement

AROUND 550 CE

Puebloan culture develops near Mesa Verde

1848

The United States gains control of all of Colorado after the Mexican-American War ends

1803

Part of Colorado is bought by the United States through the Louisiana Purchase

1858

Gold is discovered in Colorado, which leads 100,000 settlers to flock to the state

1876

Colorado becomes the 38th state to join the union

1915

Rocky Mountain National Park is officially recognized by Congress

1999

The Columbine High School massacre is the deadliest school shooting in U.S. history at the time

1893

Colorado votes to give women the right to vote, one of the first states to do so

1974

Denver schools begin to desegregate

Nicknames: Centennial State, Colorful Colorado

Motto: *Nil Sine Numine* (Nothing Without Providence)

Date of Statehood: August 1, 1876 (the 38th state)

Capital City: Denver ★

Other Major Cities: Colorado Springs, Fort Collins, Aurora, Boulder, Pueblo

Area: 104,094 square miles (269,602 square kilometers); Colorado is the 8th largest state.

Population
5,773,714
(2020)

STATE FLAG

The Colorado flag has three stripes of blue, white, and blue. In the center is a red "C" with a golden disk inside of it. The colors symbolize nature in the state. The white stands for snow on mountains, and the gold represents the state's sunshine. Red represents Colorado's soil, and the blue is a symbol of clear blue skies.

INDUSTRY

Main Exports

computers

beef

medical instruments

aircraft parts

JOBS

- MANUFACTURING **4%**
- FARMING AND NATURAL RESOURCES **4%**
- GOVERNMENT **13%**
- SERVICES **79%**

Natural Resources
coal, oil, uranium, sand, gravel

GOVERNMENT

10 ELECTORAL VOTES

Federal Government

8 REPRESENTATIVES | **2** SENATORS

USA

CO

State Government

65 REPRESENTATIVES | **35** SENATORS

STATE SYMBOLS

STATE BIRD
LARK BUNTING

STATE ANIMAL
ROCKY MOUNTAIN BIGHORN SHEEP

STATE FLOWER
COLORADO BLUE COLUMBINE

STATE TREE
COLORADO BLUE SPRUCE

amphitheatre—a round, open-air building with tiers of seats surrounding a central performance space

campuses—the grounds or buildings that make up colleges or businesses

elevation—the height above sea level

exports—products sold by one state to another state or region

farmers markets—food markets where local farmers sell the goods they grow

flash floods—sudden floods that are over quickly; flash floods are usually caused by heavy rain or melting snow.

gold rush—the rapid movement of Americans to the western part of the country after gold was discovered in the mid-1800s

Great Plains—a region of flat or gently rolling land in the central United States

heritage—the traditions, achievements, and beliefs that are part of the history of a group of people

hub—an area's center of activity

Louisiana Purchase—a deal made between France and the United States; it gave the United States 828,000 square miles (2,144,510 square kilometers) of land west of the Mississippi River.

plateau—an area of flat, raised land

service jobs—jobs that perform tasks for people or businesses

tourists—people who travel to visit another place

unemployment—the number of people who do not have jobs in an area

AT THE LIBRARY

Battista, Brianna. *Questions and Answers About the Gold Rush*. New York, N.Y.: PowerKids Press, 2019.

Kortemeier, Todd. *It's Great to Be a Fan in Colorado*. Lake Elmo, Minn.: Focus Readers, 2019.

Sommer, Nathan. *Grizzly Bear vs. Wolf Pack*. Minneapolis, Minn.: Bellwether Media, 2020.

ON THE WEB

FACTSURFER

Factsurfer.com gives you a safe, fun way to find more information.

1. Go to www.factsurfer.com.

2. Enter "Colorado" into the search box and click Q.

3. Select your book cover to see a list of related content.

INDEX

arts, 23, 25
Burro Days, 24
capital (see Denver)
challenge, 16
Chile and Frijoles Festival, 24
climate, 10, 11, 14, 22, 25
Colorado Avalanche, 23
Colorado River, 6, 7
Colorado Springs, 7, 15, 18
Colorado State Fair, 24
Denver, 6, 7, 14, 15, 16-17, 19, 23
Denver Broncos, 23
fast facts, 28-29
festivals, 24-25
food, 20-21, 24
future, 14
Great Plains, 6, 8, 10, 11, 12, 19, 20
history, 8-9, 16, 18, 21
International Snow Sculpting Championship, 25
inventions, 19
landmarks, 4, 5, 6, 18, 22, 23

landscape, 4, 5, 6, 7, 8, 10-11, 12, 17, 20
location, 6-7
Ouray Ice Festival, 25
outdoor activities, 4, 5, 22, 23, 24, 25
people, 7, 8, 9, 14-15, 21
Pueblo, 7, 24
recipe, 21
Rocky Mountain National Park, 4-5, 22
Rocky Mountains, 6, 10, 11, 12, 14, 20
Shiffrin, Mikaela, 15
size, 6
sports, 17, 22, 23, 24
timeline, 26-27
wildlife, 4, 12-13
working, 16, 18-19